Houston & New Orleans Travel Guide

Attractions, Eating, Drinking, Shopping & Places To Stay

Katherine Maxwell

Table of Contents

Houston

Houston is the largest city in Texas and the fourth largest city in the United States. It is a sprawling, cosmopolitan city inhabited by many ethnicities and nationalities. Houston is situated on the Gulf Coast of Texas and has the fourth largest port in the United States. Some of the world's leading medical and research institutions, including the Texas Medical Center and NASA's Johnson Space Center, are found in the city. Houston is second only to New York in terms of the number of Fortune 500 headquarters.

Houston attracts people from all over the world. 21% (1.1 million) of its total population were born outside the US. Latinos and Asians constitute almost two-thirds and more than one-fifth of the figure, respectively. There are 86 countries that have a consulate in Houston.

Culture

Houston is a city that is rich in culture of all types. The city offers a broad range of culinary delights from the indispensable barbeque and Tex-Mex to fantastic steakhouses and fine dining.

Shoppers can get a glimpse of Houston's riches through the Galleria's plush stores, which sell everything from high-end brands like Prada and Tiffany to rare antiques and vinyl records.

The Houston Theater, located in Downtown Houston, is home to the Alley Theater, Hobby Center for the Performing Arts, Jesse H. Jones Hall for the Performing Arts, Bayou Place and the Wortham Theater Center.

The Museum District is well-known for the Museum of Fine Arts, Houston Museum of Natural Science, the Contemporary Arts Museum Houston, the Station Museum of Contemporary Art, Holocaust Museum Houston and the Houston Zoo. Situated close to the Museum District are The Menil Collection, Rothko Chapel, and the Byzantine Fresco Chapel Museum.

The National Museum of Funeral History, which showcases famous funeral service artifacts and the original Popemobile used by Pope John Paul II, can be found near the George Bush International Airport.

Houston's rich culture goes beyond its museums and theaters. The International Festival, the Art Car Parade and the Shakespeare Festival are just some of Houston's most popular annual events.

Location & Orientation

Locations in Houston are referred to as being inside or outside Interstate 610 (also referred to as the "610 Loop" or "The Loop"). Because the area inside Interstate 610 is occupied largely by the city's business district, Houston has acquired an urbanized and sophisticated image. In Houston, the phrase "inner looper" connotes an individual who lives a cosmopolitan lifestyle.

Houston is serviced by major roadways and airports. The east-west highway US 290 intersects with Loop 610 and the Sam Houston Tollway and runs straight to the Texas capital of Austin. FM 1960 travels east, intersecting with US 290 and TX 6 in northern Harris County.

George Bush Intercontinental Airport (also known as "Intercontinental" and "Bush Intercontinental") is Houston's largest and busiest airport. Served by 17 commercial airlines and some passenger charted airlines, George Bush Intercontinental Airport facilitates more than 700 flights a day to more than 185 domestic and international destinations.

The Metropolitan Transit Authority (more popularly known as METRO) runs Houston's public transportation system. The bus and the light rail are the most common forms of public transport in Houston. METRO buses run all over Harris County and on most local roads. The METRORail runs along the following areas: Downtown, the Museum District, Hermann Park, Rice University, Houston Zoo and Reliant Park. Most bus and subway tickets cost between $2.00 and $4.50. Senior citizens receive discounted bus fares.

Climate & When to Visit

Due to its proximity to the Gulf Coast and its forests, swamps and prairies, Houston has a humid, subtropical climate. Its annual rainfall is about 48 inches and sunny days are a common occurrence.

Winters are mild in Houston. To keep warm, a light jacket would suffice. Houston's temperature in the winter is between 16 degrees Celsius and 5 degrees Celsius.

Summers in Houston can be extremely hot. A typical Houstonian summer is hottest in July — the temperature during this period can reach beyond 34 degrees Celsius. Summer mornings in Houston have a relative humidity rate of 90%, which will lower to 60% in the afternoons. Tourists visiting Houston in the summer should therefore pack summer clothes like short-sleeved shirts, shorts and sandals.

Don't worry too much about the sweltering heat—nearly all public establishments and transportation in Houston are air-conditioned.

Sightseeing Highlights

Bayou Place

500 Texas Street, Houston, TX 77002
713 227-0957

Bayou Place is a 130,000 square foot complex of
restaurants, clubs, bars and a movie theater. Opened in
1997, Bayou Place is actually the former Albert Thomas
Convention Center.

The opening of the George R. Brown Convention Center in 1987 rendered the Albert Thomas Convention Center obsolete. As a result, in 1991, Houston's city government collaborated with Maryland-based developer David Cordish to redevelop the site. Bayou Place was reopened to the public on December 31, 1997.

Bayou Place is home to some of Houston's best restaurants and entertainment establishments. A typical night out at Bayou Place begins with dinner at the renowned Hard Rock Café or the authentic Italian trattoria, Mingalone. Movie lovers can catch art and independent films at the Angelika Film Center before proceeding to the RocBar, Houston's largest "rock 'n roll"-themed nightclub, for some drinks and dancing. But the most frequented venue in Bayou Place would probably be Verizon Wireless Theater (now known as the Bayou Music Center). From 2003 to 2005, the venue was voted "Best Live Music Venue" by the *Houston Press*. Sting, Kylie Minogue, Dolly Parton and Dashboard Confessional are just some of the artists who have performed in the Verizon Wireless Theater.

Valet parking at the Bayou Place costs $3 on weekdays from 11 am to 4 pm; $8 Monday through Saturday from 4 pm to 2 am; and $8 on Sundays from 11 am to 12 pm. Self parking is available for $5-$8 at the Rusk, Capitol and Texas entrances.

Galleria Mall

5085 Westheimer Road #4850, Houston, TX 77056
713 966-3530

Galleria Mall (also known as Galleria Houston) is situated in Houston's Uptown Park section. It is likewise regarded as part of River Oaks, an upper-class community located in the central part of Houston.

The Galleria Mall is one of Houston's most popular attractions. Each year, it is visited by an estimated 24 million visitors. It has at least 375 stores, making it the seventh largest mall in the US. Its enormous size can be attributed largely to its constant expansion — it has expanded several times since it was opened in 1970.

Aside from its numerous shops, Galleria Mall also has the following facilities: an arcade, an ice skating rink, office towers, two Westin hotels and restaurants that range from the popular Ninfa's Mexican Restaurant chain to the themed Rainforest Café chain. Galleria Mall is a shopper's paradise. It has it all, from designer brands like Gucci Neiman Marcus and Cartier to makeup and videogame consoles. Whatever a shopper needs, Galleria Mall surely has it all.

Johnson Space Center (NASA)

2101 NASA Parkway #1, Houston, TX 77058
281 483-0123
http://www.spacecenter.org

The Lyndon B. Johnson Space Center (formerly known as the Manned Spacecraft Center) is one of NASA's nine field installations and is the home base for US astronauts. A 1600-acre site, located 30 miles south of Houston, the Johnson Space Center is composed of 142 buildings that house NASA's facilities for carrying out space operations and applied research.

Visitors can experience how it feels to live in a zero-gravity environment in the Living in Space Exhibit or witness a simulated rocket launch (complete with exhaust) at the Blast Off! Theater. The NASA Tram Tour provides tourists a first-hand view of where real astronauts work. The tour showcases real NASA facilities that astronauts use in their space missions. Trams seat 100 people (seats are wheelchair accessible) and are available on a first-come, first-served basis.

The Space Shuttle Mock-Up allows tourists to personally experience the feeling of being inside an actual space shuttle. The Space Shuttle Mock-Up is a replica of the space shuttle's flight deck and mid-deck, designed by astronaut Charles Bolden. Tourists can step inside the mock-up, giving them an opportunity to see where and how astronauts live and work while in space. The Space Shuttle Mock-Up is open continuously on normal days.

The Astronaut Gallery has the best collection of space suits from all over the world. Behind the Astronaut Gallery is a "Wall of Fame" that exhibits the portraits and profiles of every US astronaut who has been to outer space.

Houston Zoo

6200 Hermann Park Drive,
Houston, TX 77030
713 533-6500
http://www.houstonzoo.org

Houston Zoo is found inside Hermann Park, one of the most-visited public parks in Houston.

With a size of about 22 hectares, Houston Zoo serves as a sanctuary to more than 6,000 animals from at least 9,000 species. It is the seventh most-visited zoo in the US, its visitors reaching an estimated 1.6 million yearly.

The Reptile and Amphibian Building is the Houston Zoo's main reptile and amphibian resource. It showcases at least 300 species, as well as one of the world's 14 leucistic American alligator displays. The John P. McGovern Children's Zoo offers children a glimpse of native Texan wildlife. Some examples of its displays are bald eagles, bats and prairie dogs living in reconstructed habitats. It also has domesticated animals like goats and cows for petting.

Those interested in animal conversion efforts should go to the Janice Suber McNair Asian Elephant Habitat. This facility is home to the following elephants: adult bull Thai, adult cows Methai, Shanti, and Tess, juvenile bull Tucker (Tess' son), and calves Baylor (Shanti's son) and Tupelo (Tess' daughter). Opened in 2008, the Janice Suber McNair Asian Elephant Habitat was renovated in 2011 to include these facilities: a bigger display area, a pool that could accommodate several elephants, new explanatory notices, and a quarter for demonstration of mating behaviors.

Museum District

1401 Richmond Avenue #290,
Houston, TX 77006
713 715-1939
http://houstonmuseumdistrict.org

The Museum District collectively refers to the 19 museums located within a 1.5-mile radius of Houston's Hermann Park.

Asia Society Texas Center

The Asia Society Texas Center is a venue for activities that would promote pan-Asian art, culture, business, education and government policy. It is open from Tuesday to Saturday from 11 am to 6 pm. Asia Society members are entitled to free admission to exhibitions; non-members are required to pay $5.00.

Children's Museum

The Children's Museum of Houston is filled with fun and educational activities and exhibits for children. FlowWorks allows children to personally experience how it feels to become a plumber or an engineer by letting them inspect, operate and maintain certain hydraulic facilities. The Invention Convention is a workshop that allows children to come up with their own inventions.

Matter Factory exhibits materials and information related to science and nanotechnology. The Children's Museum of Houston is open from Tuesday to Saturday from 10 am to 6 pm. On Thursdays, it is open from 10 am to 8 pm. On Saturdays, it is open from noon to 6 pm. Admission costs $9 per person and $8 for seniors aged 65 and older. The Free Family Night (the museum's free hours) takes place on Thursdays from 5 pm to 8 pm and every first Sunday of the month from noon to 6 pm.

Holocaust Museum

The Holocaust Museum Houston is dedicated to the victims and survivors of the Holocaust. It shows information, artworks, films and artifacts related to the Holocaust and more recent genocides. The Holocaust Museum is open from 9 am to 5 pm on weekdays and from noon to 5 pm on weekends (admission is always free). Every first Thursday of the month, the museum is open from 5 pm to 8 pm.

Center for Contemporary Craft

Crafts lovers will surely enjoy visiting the Houston Center for Contemporary Craft (HCCC). The HCCC is a non-profit arts group that opened in September 2001. It aims to promote crafts and craft education. It focuses extensively on artworks made from clay, fiber, glass, metal wood and recycled materials.

The HCCC is currently one of the leading cultural and educational facilities both in Houston and the Southwest. It is also one of the few establishments in the US that is centered exclusively on craft. It supports local and national artists by providing studio spaces, staging exhibits and facilitating the sale of artworks. Moreover, HCCC conducts educational and outreach activities for thousands of children each year.

HCCC allows visitors to see the entire creative process, from why an artist decided to come up with a certain artwork to how that artwork was done. The Craft Garden, located at the back of the HCCC building, shows how plant materials are grown and processed into clothing items like jeans and t-shirts. The Artist Hall, the HCCC's wing of artist studios, shares information about and conducts live demonstrations of specific types of crafts. The Asher Gallery, the HCCC's in-house gift shop, sells artworks done by local and national artists.

The HCCC is open from 10 am to 5 pm from Tuesday to Saturday. On Sundays, it is open from noon to 5 pm (except on Labor Day weekend). Admission is free.

Contemporary Arts Museum

Founded in 1948, the Contemporary Arts Museum Houston showcases the best contemporary art (art in the last 40 years) in the US and abroad. True to its nature, it resides in the Houston Museum District's landmark stainless steel building (designed by esteemed architect Gunnar Bikerts).

The museum aims to educate the public regarding the role of art in modern life through lectures, exhibits, original publications and instructive programs. Tourists will certainly have a fun time shopping at the Museum Shop, the Contemporary Arts Museum Houston's in-site gift shop. The shop has a huge rage of unusual gifts, from books about contemporary art to contemporary art-themed toys for children.

The Contemporary Arts Museum Houston is open from Tuesday to Sunday at these times: 10 am to 7 pm (Tuesday, Wednesday and Friday), 10 am to 9 pm (Thursday), 10 am to 6 pm (Saturday) and 12 pm to 6 pm (Sunday). Admission is free.

Czech Center Museum

The Czech Center Museum intends to celebrate and preserve Bohemian, Moravian, Silesian and Slovakian arts and culture. The museum is a beautiful Baroque-style building that displays antique furniture, toys, dolls, figurines, traditional costumes, Bohemian and Czech crystal, porcelain and ceramics, antique jewelry, paintings and Moravian hand-painted pottery.

The museum conducts activities like exhibits, concerts, lectures and language classes. Other facilities include genealogy research and library facilities, an ecumenical chapel, a grand ballroom, business rooms and Prague International Gifts, a gift shop that sells unique Czech and Bohemian collectibles.

The Czech Center Museum is open from Monday to Saturday from 10 am to 4 pm. Admission costs $6 per person and $3 for children.

Museum of Fine Arts

The Museum of Fine Arts Houston (MFAH) is the fifth largest museum in the US and the first art museum in Texas (it was opened in 1924). Measuring about 300,000 square feet, the MFAH houses over 40,000 pieces of artwork from six continents, as well as seven facilities, including the Caroline Wiess Law Building, the Glassell School of Art and the Bayou Bend Collections and Garden (the former home of famed Texas philanthropist Ima Hogg). Each year, the MFAH is visited by at least 1.25 million people.

The MFAH is open from Tuesday to Sunday at the following times: 10 am to 5 pm (Tuesday and Wednesday), 10 am to 9 pm (Thursday), 10 am to 7 pm (Friday and Saturday) and 12:15 pm to 7 pm (Sunday). Admission costs $7 per person, $3.50 for seniors and children and free for children below 5 years old and on Thursdays.

Health Museum

The Health Museum Houston is one of Houston's most interactive museums. Each year, more than 180,000 tourists come to this museum to have a close-up look at the various parts of the human body, as well as how it works.

Some of the Health Museum Houston's highlights are: You: The Exhibit (a body scanner that provides real-time images of a person's body), the Amazing Body Pavilion (a giant, walk-in model of the human body) and the McGovern 4-D Theater (Houston's first 4-D theater). In fact, the Amazing Body Pavilion has giant human teeth displays that tourists can actually sit on.

The Health Museum Houston is open all week at these times: 9 am to 5 pm (Monday to Saturday) and 12 noon to 5 pm (Sunday). Admission costs $8 per person, $6 for seniors and children 3 to 12 years old and free for children below 2 years old and on Thursdays from 2 to 7 pm.

Houston Center for Photography (HCP)

The Houston Center for Photography (HCP) displays timely and relevant photography and photojournalism done by both up-and-coming and recognized photographers. Since its inception in 1981, the HCP has exhibited the work of about 3,200 photographers and trained countless others.

Its most recent exhibits include a photo essay detailing the 60-year history of Magnum Photos (the most celebrated photography cooperative in the world) and the impact of conflict in the Middle East in the US. Every year, the HCP stages the Print Auction Exhibition, a free-to-attend auction of works donated by some of the world's most excellent photographers.

The HCP is the only institution in the South and the Southwest that offers year-round courses on photography and other visual arts. These courses are made up of more than 200 classes on various subjects, from basic photography to photographic technology. The HCP's learning facilities include a high-tech digital darkroom, film editing software and a library stocked with over 2,000 photography books.

The HCP also believes in using photography as a means to give back to the community. Once a year, the center enables economically disadvantaged high school students and young cancer patients at M.D. Anderson Cancer Center to illustrate their plights through photography. The HCP will then stage an exhibit to showcase their works. The HCP is open from Wednesday to Saturday. Admission and parking (in the HCP parking lot) is always free.

Lawndale Art Center

Situated just one block from the Houston Center for Contemporary Craft, the Lawndale Art Center is an art deco-style building that houses four galleries, which host a total of more than 20 exhibits each year. Unlike other art museums in the Houston Museum District, the Lawndale Art Center is focused solely on promoting the works of Houston artists. The center likewise hosts several special occasions, including *Dia de los Muertos* (Day of the Dead) and the annual 20th Century Modern Market (the center's yearly sale of twentieth-century artworks). The Lawndale Art Center is open from Monday to Saturday. Admission is always free, except for admission to the 20th Century Modern Market.

Museum of Natural Science

The Houston Museum of Natural Science can be likened to a science encyclopedia — it has permanent displays on almost every branch of natural science, from dinosaurs to astronomy and space. At any given time, however, the museum conducts two or three special exhibits that are sometimes not related to the natural sciences. One example is the set of gifts designed for, given to and used by Tibet's Dalai Lamas over the past nine centuries.

Aside from exhibits, the Houston Museum of Natural Science also has several learning centers. The Burke Baker Planetarium allows tourists to view constellations, as well as to watch and listen to science-themed movies and music. The Cockrell Butterfly Center, the museum's butterfly sanctuary, is a virtual rainforest that includes a 50-foot waterfall and exotic plants. Brown Hall, a facility found inside the Cockrell Butterfly Center, houses spiders and live insects such as walking sticks, cockroaches and tarantulas.

Visitors can learn more about insects in the museum's "Insects and Us" section. Here, they can learn how to make their own butterfly garden, keep bees and ward off mosquitoes. There are also insect-themed toys and books for children. Strollers, however, are not allowed in the Cockrell Butterfly Center — butterflies can sometimes get inside them.

And in order to be able to reach out and educate more people, especially the youth, the Houston Museum of Natural Science decided to open two satellite educational campuses. The **Woodlands Xploration Stadium**, situated in the northern part of Houston, showcases 13 dinosaur skeletons, live frogs and various minerals and gems. The George Observatory, located in the southern part of Houston, has three domed telescopes, including the Gueymard Research Telescope. At 36 inches, it is one of the largest telescopes in the US that is open to the public. Aside from its massive telescopes, the George Observatory also houses the Challenger Learning Center. The Challenger Learning Center uses simulated missions as a means of teaching tourists about science and space explorations.

The Houston Museum of Natural Science is open all week. Admission costs $15 for adults, $9 for college students, seniors 62 years old and up and children between 3 to 11 years old. Learning centers, however, may charge additional fees. Admission to the Cockrell Butterfly Center requires an additional $8 ticket purchase. Admission to the Burke Baker Planetarium requires an additional $7. But admission to these two learning centers will cost only $6 for students, seniors and children below 11 years old.

John C. Freeman Weather Museum

The John C. Freeman Weather Museum is the only museum in the US that is focused on the weather. The Weather Research Center, a Houston-based non-profit organization that aims to raise public awareness about weather and weather safety, founded the said museum in 2006. The Weather Research Center runs the John C. Freeman Weather Museum to this day.

The museum is very popular with children mainly because of its several hands-on activities. They can record their own weather forecast in a virtual studio, see meteorologists conduct experiments in the Weather Wizard Corner or touch a computer-generated tornado vortex in the Tornado Chamber. Tourists can also get to know the history of meteorology, find out how tornadoes form and how satellite images of previous hurricanes like Katrina and Rita can be used to track hurricanes.

The John C. Freeman Weather Museum is open from Monday to Saturday. Admission costs $5 for adults, $3 for students and seniors and is free for children below three years old. But a guided tour will cost $8 for adults and $5 for students, teachers and seniors. A guided tour lasts between an hour and an hour-and-a-half and must be booked in advance by phone.

Kemah Boardwalk

215 Kipp Avenue, Kemah, TX 77565
877 285-3624
http://www.kemahboardwalk.com

Kemah Boardwalk is a 42-acre hotel and restaurant complex located 20 miles from downtown Houston. It has numerous waterfront restaurants, amusement establishments and retail stores, as well as festivals and daily seaside shows.

Landry's Seafood House, the Cadillac Bar, and Saltgrass Steakhouse are just some of the dining options available in Kemah Boardwalk. There are likewise theme park attractions such as a Ferris wheel, train ride and a carousel. But the most popular attraction in Kemah Boardwalk would probably be the 140-passenger speedboat called the Boardwalk Beast. The Boardwalk Beast is a 70-foot (21 m) open-deck speedboat that runs for up to 40 miles per hour (64 km/h). Its passengers will surely enjoy a wild, wet 25-minute ride out into Galveston Bay. Boardwalk Beast rides are available from Spring Break until Thanksgiving.

Accommodation is not a problem at Kemah Boardwalk — tourists can stay at the Boardwalk Inn. Despite having the ambiance of a seaside cottage, the Boardwalk Inn boasts of complete and modern amenities. It has corporate rooms and a ballroom for special functions such as weddings, anniversaries and business conferences. There are likewise several shops, restaurants and amusement centers within walking distance of the Boardwalk Inn.

Splashtown

21300 Interstate 45,
Spring, TX 77373
281 355-3300
http://www.splashtownpark.com/

Splashtown is a water park situated in the northern part of Houston. It is a family-oriented water park that has attractions for guests of all ages. Children will certainly enjoy Crocodile Isle, a play area that has fully interactive facilities like a pirate ship and slides. Guests can rent a cabana for at least $75 (the rate can go up depending on the day of rental and the amenities included). The rental fee already covers tickets, food and beverage wait service, meals, towels, a family-sized locker and more for up to four guests. Discounted rates apply to groups of 15 or more. Ticket orders must be placed at least 3 weeks in advance.

Montrose Neighborhood

Montrose, Houston

Montrose is one of the best examples of Houston's cultural diversity. It practically has a sliver of everything, from restored mansions and bungalows to gay and lesbian activism. Montrose is home to the following city-designated historical districts: Courtlandt Place (1996), Westmoreland (1997), Avondale East (1999), Avondale West (2007), and Audubon Place (2009). Existing architectural styles include Victorian, Queen Anne, Prairie, American Four Square, Craftsman, Bungalow, Mission, Colonial and Tudor Revival. The former homes of eccentric millionaire Howard Hughes and former US President Lyndon B. Johnson are located in Montrose.

Despite Montrose's old-world charm, it is also a vibrant retail and entertainment destination. From high-end boutiques to thrift shops, Montrose has it all. As of 2012, there were about 200 restaurants in Montrose, some of which are ethnic restaurants, tea and coffee shops, delis and bakeries, and fast-food restaurants. Montrose also has several dance clubs, dive bars and alternative lounges, many of which are open 27/7.

Montrose has a wide array of art galleries and museums. The Menil Collection contains artworks from various cultures around the world, as well as from various historical periods. Art League Houston is a origami-inspired building that exhibits contemporary art in a variety of media and conducts classes on printmaking, jewelry, painting in a variety of media and styles, drawing, and collage, among others.

Montrose is the center of Houston's Lesbian, Gay, Bisexual and Transgender (LGBT) community. The latter has wielded considerable political and economic clout over Montrose for decades. In fact, as of 2009, Montrose had the tenth highest number of households run by same-sex couples in the US.

Downtown Aquarium

410 Bagby Street, Houston, TX 77002
713 223-3474
http://www.aquariumrestaurants.com/downtownaquariumhouston/

Downtown Aquarium was developed from two Downtown Houston landmarks: Fire Station No. 1 and the Central Waterworks Building. It is currently a 500,000-gallon aquatic wonderland that houses more than 200 species of marine life from various parts of the world. Guests can see swimming white tigers, pet a stingray or ride a train straight through the Shark Voyage.

At the same time, Downtown Aquarium is a splendid six-acre entertainment and dining complex. It has a full-service restaurant, an upscale bar, a fully equipped ballroom, aquatic and geographic exhibits, shops and a variety of amusement facilities. One of Downtown Aquarium's most popular rides is its 100-feet carousel — the carousel's highest point provides riders an impressive view of the Houston skyline.

Downtown Aquarium has many educational programs for children and young people. One of these programs is the Sea Safari Summer Camp, a learning camp for students from 9 to 13 years old. The camp teaches them interesting facts about ocean life and has fun games and crafts. Downtown Aquarium's exhibits are open from 10 am to 9 pm from Monday to Thursday, 10 am to 11 pm on Fridays and Saturdays and 10 am to 9 pm on Sundays. The restaurants are open from 11 am to 9 pm from Monday to Thursday, 11 am to 11 pm on Fridays and Saturdays and 11 am to 9 pm on Sundays. A ticket to the aquarium exhibits costs $9.25 (adults), $8.25 (seniors aged 65 and above) and $6.25 (children 2-12 years old). Children under two years old can enter for free.

Old Town Spring

403 Main Street Spring, TX 77373
281 353-9310
http://www.oldtownspring.com/

Old Town Spring is a turn-of-the century town found north of Houston and outside Beltway 8. True to its name, it is composed of early 19th-century style shops, restaurants, museums and art galleries. Tourists will definitely feel like they "travelled back in time" when they go through Old Town Spring's nearly 150 shops, which sell merchandise ranging from Amish furniture to Shabby Chic home accents. After a nostalgic window shopping experience, tourists can catch a live gig at the Jailhouse Saloon.

Accommodation facilities at the Old Town Spring are composed of two hotels and an RV resort. The Rayford Crossing RV Resort is a full-service resort with facilities that include heated pools, gamerooms, a spa and a pet park. Tourists can rent a fully-furnished cabin for at least $92 a day.

Recommendations for the Budget Traveler

Places to Stay

Hotel Derek Houston Galleria

2525 West Loop South, Houston, TX 77027
713 961-3000
http://www.hotelderek.com

The Hotel Derek Houston Galleria is adjacent to the Galleria Mall, the Uptown entertainment district and the Texas Medical Center.

Its amenities include a fully-stocked minibar, hairdryer, coffee and tea marker, iron and ironing board, large in-room safe and DVD players. Each room has high-speed Internet access, a dual-line phone, private voicemail, cable television and FedEx supplies available at the front desk. Accommodation begins at $76 per night.

Royal Sonesta Hotel

2222 West Loop South Houston, TX 77027
713 627-7600
http://www.sonesta.com/RoyalHouston/

The Royal Sonesta Hotel Houston is only a few blocks from the Galleria Mall. It is located near the Museum and Theater districts, and just minutes from Downtown Houston. Its amenities include a 24-hour health club, outdoor swimming pool, 24-hour in-room food delivery service, high-speed Internet access and concierge service. Each room has high-speed Internet access (wired and wireless), two dual-line telephones with voicemail, laptop-size electronic safe, minibar and coffee and tea makers. Accommodation begins at $44 per night.

Baymont Inn & Suites

9902 Gulf Freeway, Houston, TX 77001
713 941-0900
http://www.baymontinns.com/hotels/texas/houston/baymont-inn-and-suites-houston-sam-houston-parkway/hotel-overview

Baymont Inn & Suites Houston is located at Beltway 8. It is near the George Washington Interncontinental Airport, Patterson Drilling, Varco, Schlumberger and RPC. Its amenities include indoor and outdoor pools, gym, outdoor patio space and a business center (for meetings and conferences). Guests enjoy free continental breakfast and rooms that have free Wi-Fi Internet access and a 32-inch flat-panel TV. Accommodation begins at $38 per night (kids 17 and under stay free with an adult).

Super 8 Intercontinental

7010 Will Clayton Parkway, Humble, TX 77338
281 446-5100
http://www.super8.com/hotels/texas/humble/super-8-intercontinental-houston-tx/hotel-overview

Super 8 Intercontinental Houston is only minutes from Route 59, George Bush Intercontinental Airport and Space Center Houston. Its amenities include an outdoor pool, guest laundry facilities and handicapped-accessible and non-smoking rooms. Guests enjoy a free continental breakfast and free high-speed Internet. Accommodation begins at $47 (kids 17 and under stay free with an adult).

Four Points by Sheraton Houston Southwest

2828 Southwest Freeway, Houston, TX 77098
713 942-2111

Four Points by Sheraton Houston Southwest is located between Downtown Houston and the Galleria Mall. Its amenities include a Business Center that has the following: High Speed Internet Access, two Mac computers and two laser printers (fees apply). Additional business services such as faxing, copying and document scanning available at the Front Desk for a small fee. Each room has high-speed Internet access, free bottled water, in-room movie and in-room dining. Accommodation begins at $69.

Places to Eat

Empire Café

1732 Westheimer Road, Houston, TX 77098
713 528-5282
http://www.empirecafe.com

Located between Montrose and Shepherd, Empire Café is a European-style café that serves breakfast, appetizers, soups, salads, lunch, dinner, desserts and drinks.

The breakfast menu is composed of omelets and other egg recipes that can be served with a side dish of sausages, toast, ham, bacon, muffin, hash browns, baked potato or scones. Pancakes, hot cereal and waffles are also available. Empire Café's appetizer, soup, salad, lunch and dinner options are made up of Italian dishes such as pasta and pizza. Desserts are made up of various cakes and cookies. Side dishes are priced between $1.45 and $2.95. Meals may vary between $3.95 and $10.95. Drinks (coffee, beer, juice and wine) cost between $1.95 and $27.

Ruggles Cafe Bakery

2365 Rice Boulevard, Houston, TX
713 520-6662
http://www.rugglescafebakery.com

The Ruggles Café Bakery is an award-winning bakery that also serves homemade soups, fresh sandwiches and salads, hearty pastas and freshly-baked desserts. Some of the house specialties include Grilled Chicken Mango Salad, Beer-battered Fish Tacos and Fusilli Pasta with Shrimp. A Children's Menu (for children aged 12 years old and under) is also available. Expect to pay between $1.95 and $12.95.

Oishii Japanese Restaurant & Sushi Bar

3764 Richmond Avenue, Houston, TX 77046
832 539-4178
http://www.oishiihouston.com/menu.aspx

Oishii Japanese Restaurant & Sushi Bar serves appetizers, lunch and dinner. It also has a "Happy Hour" from Monday to Saturday. The menu is made up of Japanese staples like sushi, tempura and Udon noodles. Expect to pay between $1.25 and $29.95.

Crave Cupcakes

1151-06 Uptown Park Boulevard Houston, TX 77056
713 622-7283
http://www.cravecupcakes.com/

Crave Cupcakes is a cupcake lover's paradise. It has a wide assortment of cupcakes, from dark chocolate to gluten-free. Each cupcake costs at least $2.50. Coffee is also available.

Bubba's Texas Burger Shack

5230 Westpark Drive, Houston, TX 77056
713 661-1622
http://www.bubbastexasburgershack.com

Bubba's Texas Burger Shack is popularly known as "Home of the Buffalo Burger." For the past 25 years, this small restaurant has been serving hamburgers made from buffalo meat. The menu also includes Tex-Mex specialties like chili stuffed potatoes, frito pie and jalapeno potato salad. Meals may vary between $3.25 and $9.50. Bubba's Texas Burger Shack likewise sells souvenir items like t-shirts and sauces.

Places to Shop

Harwin Drive

Situated in the southwest part of Houston, Harwin Drive is a maze of warehouse stores. Harwin Drive is sometimes regarded as the secret of some of Houston's most fashionable women. This is because the shops on Harwin Drive sell the same merchandise that Houston's high-end boutiques sell for half the price. In fact, many high-end stores in Houston buy merchandise from Harwin Drive, mark it up and then sell it back to consumers.

Sand Dollar Thrift Store

Yale Street,
Houston, TX 77008
(713) 923-1461 1903

Sand Dollar Thrift Store is a gigantic shop found in Houston Heights. Despite its dusty and run-down appearance, it is a bargain hunter's paradise. It sells tons of clothes ranging from vintage to modern for cheap prices.

Blue Bird Circle

615 West Alabama Street,
Houston, TX 77006
(713) 528-5607

Blue Bird Circle is one of Houston's oldest thrift shops — it has been selling secondhand merchandise since 1959. Although Blue Bird Circle sells slightly-used clothing and furniture for reduced prices, it still marks down merchandise that has remained unsold for some time already. Forty percent of its consignment sales are donated to worthy causes like the Texas Children's Hospital's Blue Bird Circle Clinic for Pediatric Neurology.

Value Village

311 19th Street (at Rutland),
Houston, TX 77008
(713) 685-5440

True to its name, Value Village sells "value-for-money" merchandise. It has racks and racks of non-designer clothing for very cheap prices. Its non-clothing merchandise includes vintage jewelry, Texas high school coffee mugs and velvet paintings.

Salvation Army Store

2208 Washington Ave.,
Houston, TX 77007
(713) 425-8727

Bookworms on a budget will like shopping at the Salvation Army Store. Wednesday is "Half-Price Day".

New Orleans

New Orleans is the crossroads of old world elegance and new world frivolity. The Big Easy is a patchwork of cultures and a seat of artistic innovation. Jazz was born here. Creole cuisine was perfected here. Beautiful and iconic neighborhoods are stitched together to form New Orleans including the popular French Quarter and world famous Bourbon Street.

New Orleans is one of America's most popular tourist attractions. The aftermath of the 2005 hurricane Katrina left the city battered, but not beaten. Today its population is lower than prior to the devastating floods, but the most frequently visited sections of the city along the Mississippi river were never flooded. The central parts of the city are recovering well.

History comes alive in New Orleans. The art and architecture of Europe, Africa, and the Caribbean all jockey for attention with the city's rich traditions of food, music and good times.

New Orleans is host to several historical places and museums, including Fort Pike, the National World War II Museum, and the New Orleans Historic Voodoo Museum.

Many visitors come to New Orleans to see the French Quarter and Bourbon Street. But each neighborhood has its own individual style and attractions.

Culture

Any New Orleanian can tell you the only rule here is "Laissez les bons temps rouler", or "Let the good times roll". True to its nickname, the Big Easy is relaxed and informal. The different peoples that have called New Orleans home in the past 300 years made it a unique and joyous place.

New Orleans is most famous for the famous annual Mardi Gras. This festival has roots in European Catholicism; it's a pre-Lent party. But, Carnival New Orleans-style pulls elements from its various people's traditions, with elements from African, Caribbean and Native American traditions.

Live music is everywhere you go in the cradle the Crescent City. Live bands play in bars, clubs, and street corners. The French Quarter is especially loaded with performing musicians. Not everyone is playing Jazz, although there is plenty of that to be found. Every style of music form calypso to classical and from hip-hop to rock can be found any day of the week.

Fine art and crafts are available to view in the many museums, including the New Orleans Museum of Art (NOMA). Art can also be purchased from local artists along the many shops that line the streets of this cultural boomtown. Like her people, the art of this city have roots all over the world.

Location & Orientation

The city of New Orleans sits on a bend on the banks of the mighty Mississippi River, hence the name "Crescent City". The city occupies the Mississippi River Delta south of Lake Pontchartrain. The city is a little over a hundred miles (161 kilometers) north of the Gulf of Mexico. The city sits about six feet (1.8 meters) below see level.

The proximity to the Mississippi River and Lake Pontchartrain, along with its low elevation, subject New Orleans subject to flooding. The city is crisscrossed with levees and other flood control edifices.

The city is not laid out in a grid pattern. Most of the streets radiate outward from the center of the older part of the city. Canal Street is the traditional dividing line between the "downtown" and "uptown" areas. Locals usually make reference to nearby water features when describing locations. Points of interest may be lakeside or riverside. Louis Armstrong New Orleans International Airport is about fifteen miles from downtown.

Three streetcar lines serve the more popular areas of New Orleans. Other areas are served by a bus system. A separate bus system serves the Jefferson Parrish area. The fares for a bus and streetcar are typically $1.25; express service is available for $1.50. Taxicab service is also available, but is much costlier than streetcar or bus service.

Climate & When to Visit

The best time to visit depends on your feelings about Marti Gras. If you love a festive atmosphere the city is in full time party mode from February through May. This is also the peak tourist season. In addition to Mardi Gras, there are many other celebrations this time of year, including St. Patrick's Day and St. Joseph's Day.

January, on average, is the coolest month with an average high of 62 degrees Fahrenheit (17 degrees Celsius) and an average low of 43 degrees Fahrenheit (7 degrees Celsius). July and August are the hottest months with an average high of 91 degrees Fahrenheit (34 degrees Celsius) and an average low of 74 degrees Fahrenheit (24 degrees Celsius).

The high heat and sweltering humidity make June to September the off-season for most visitors. However, this is also the time of year to get the best deals on hotel rooms and airfare.

October is the driest month of the year and June is the wettest month. Hurricane season begins June 1st and continues until the middle of November. September is typically the most active month for Atlantic hurricanes.

Sightseeing Highlights

Mardi Gras

French Quarter

"Mardi Gras" comes from French. It literally means Fat Tuesday. This phrase technically refers to the last day of Carnival. In the United States Mardi Gras is often meant to refer to the entire Carnival season. The festivities in New Orleans begin on January 5th, also known as Twelfth Night, and last through Fat Tuesday, with the two weeks before Ash Wednesday seeing the greatest number of parades, parties, and coloured beads.

New Orleans has its own set of unique Mardi Gras traditions that set it apart from other Carnival celebrations all over the world. There are parades, thrown by various "krewes" every night during the two-week lead up to Mardi Gras. Some of the better know krewes are Rex, Zulu, and Orpheus. Rex dates back to 1872. Orpheus is much newer and was started by Harry Connick Jr. It is also the largest krewe.

This is a party city and Mardi Gras is the biggest party of the year. There is plenty of alcohol-fuelled revelry and a fair amount of debauchery. Bourbon Street and the French Quarter are the best-known places to watch parades and to participate in one of the world's greatest street parties.

As strange as it may sound, Mardi Gras can be for families too. Parades can be found all over the city. Many local families take their children to watch the parades. One tradition is to bring ladders to the parade for children to sit on. Krewes toss trinkets called "throws" to parade watchers as they pass. The trinkets are often beads, but can be anything from small toys to coins.

Many of the big parades follow established routes through Midtown and the French Quarter. The routes and times are well published in local brochures, newspapers, and online.

Part of the fun of Mardi Gras is stumbling upon many of the smaller parades, Mardi Gras Indians, and roaming bands not published like the major parades. What's a party without spontaneity? Feel free to wear a mask, try some king cakes, and call for some throws.

Bourbon Street

French Quarter

This avenue can be thought of as Mardi Gras central. It is part of the parade route for all of the major parades. People who don't know anything else about the city or Mardi Gras know that Bourbon Street is the place to go if you want to party.

The party on Bourbon Street is not reserved for Mardi Gras. The street is lined with hotels, bars, and restaurants. The entire street is blocked off to traffic at night. Most locals avoid this street, but most tourists can't say they've seen New Orleans unless they visited Bourbon Street.

Bourbon Street is located in the historic French Quarter. It's reputation as a centre of debauchery does back more than two hundred years. Legend has it that Jazz began becoming popular when pioneering impresarios like King Oliver and Jelly Roll Morton started performing in the brothels of Bourbon Street.

Today Bourbon Street is lined with souvenir shops and major corporations own some of the premises. However, Bourbon Street is still as wild as ever, definitely not a family friendly venue, especially after dark.

Historic Voodoo Museum

724 Dumaine Street
New Orleans, LA 70116
Tel: 504 680 0128

New Orleans has no shortage of museums. But the French Quarter's Historic Voodoo Museum is one of the most unique. This museum is located in the historic French Quarter between Bourbon Street and Royal Street.

Voodoo is found through out Africa and the Caribbean. Voodoo in New Orleans is unique from the practices found elsewhere in the world. It was influenced, like everything else in this city, by the diversity of people living in and around New Orleans. Voodoo has its routes in the religious practices of several tribes originating in West Africa.

The slave trade brought practitioners of this ancient religion to New Orleans. Creole, French, and Spanish customs and religions, influenced their traditions. Voodoo as found in New Orleans is heavily influenced by Catholicism as well as Creole traditions.

This museum is not large, but it is packed with voodoo artifacts, including voodoo dolls, gris-gris (a voodoo amulet), and other voodoo charms. The museum traces the history and practices of Voodoo in New Orleans. A guided tour is available.

The museum also explains the place of zombies, Voodoo Queens, and gris-gris to New Orleans and New Orleans Voodoo. Often there is a Voodoo Priest or Priestess onsite willing to give a psychic reading for a price.

The museum is open seven days a week and is open from 10:00 am to at least 6:00 pm. General admission is $7. Discounts are available for seniors, military personnel, and students.

Hermann-Grima House

820 Saint Louis Street
New Orleans, LA 70156
Tel: 504 525 5661

German Jewish immigrant Samuel Hermann built this French Quarter stalwart in 1831. This Federal style house also includes a restored private stable and working Creole kitchen, complete with open hearth.

October through May is the best time to visit this National Historic Landmark. Open-hearth cooking demonstrations occur daily during these months. The guided tours provide not only a history of the mansion and grounds, but use the mansion to put New Orleans history in perspective.

Everyone working at this historical masterpiece knows the history of the house and the city. Staffers dress in period costume. The house itself is furnished with painstaking accuracy and attention to detail.

Prior to visiting call ahead and check the tour hours. Sometime tours are not offered in the late afternoon. Admission is $12. Senior, student, military and AAA discounts are available.

St. Louis Cathedral

615 Pere Antoine Alley
New Orleans, LA 70116
Tel: 504 525 9585

Overlooking vibrant Jackson Square and the mighty Mississippi River in the heart of the French Quarter, is the oldest continuously operating cathedral in the United States. Officially known as The Cathedral-Basilica of Saint Louis, King of France, St. Louis Cathedral offers a welcome change of pace to some of the city's rowdier attractions.

A church has been on this site since 1727. The original building burned down and was rebuilt from 1789 to 1794. The building was significantly renovated in 1844. The church bell from 1815 still peals the hours from above the church's clock.

The art and décor are worth the visit. The church contains marvellous stained glass scenes from the life of Louis IX, King of France. The interior also contains murals and a statue of Joan of Arc.

Hurricane Katrina damaged the remarkable cathedral. Leaks in the roof damaged the pipe organ, which has since been restored. A statue of Jesus, outside the basilica, lost a thumb and forefinger. In a moving sermon, the archbishop of the time, Archbishop Hughes, declared that the statue would not be repaired until New Orleans was healed from the wounds of Katrina,

This history and beauty of this sight make it a must see for both religious and secular visitors. The tour guides are friendly and knowledgeable. The church makes a nice sanctuary from the oppressive summer sun. Admission is free.

Jackson Square

French Quarter

Historic buildings ring this grand public square. St. Louis Cathedral and two Spanish colonial style buildings, one of which, the Cabildo, was the sight where the Louisiana Purchase treaty was signed, line one side of the square. Around the square can also be found the Faulkner House, the place where William Faulkner wrote his first novel, and Pontalba Buildings, among the oldest continuously rented residences in the United States.

A large statue of the hero of the battle of New Orleans from the war of 1812, Andrew Jackson, stands in the middle of the square. This large public square is about more than just history.

Artists have displayed and sold their work in and around the square for over a hundred years. Visitors today can watch pastel portrait masters and painters at work any day of the year.

The square also has its share of fortune-tellers, occasional wedding celebrations, and traveling showman. Frequent brass marching bands are a favourite attraction. A former archbishop of nearby St. Louis Cathedral remarked that it was the only place a bishop could enter the church to the sounds of "When the Saints Go Marching In".

Around the square are several restaurants and cafes. A hungry traveller won't have trouble finding a beignet or other confection to satisfy a craving.

There is no fee to enter the square. Horse and mule drawn cabs and carriages are available for hire.

French Market

1008 North Peters Street
New Orleans, LA 70116
Tel: 504 522 2621

A New Orleans version of a European market, the French Market is six blocks of shopping. Much of the area has been dedicated to shopping since 1791, when a Native American trading post was established. Some of the buildings date as far back as 1813.

Items from farmer's produce to tourist trap bric-a-brac can be found in the open-air market and shops of the French Market. Restaurants and food stalls dot the French Market with selections from all over the world. Many delicious examples of both Cajun and Creole cuisine can be sampled here.

The Farmers Market portion can be found near Jackson Square. In addition to having a variety of produce for sale, visitors can also pick-up any number of crafts and sample food from a variety of eateries. There is a French Market Fare stage where everything from cooking demonstrations to music performances are held.

The French Market Flea Market is at the other end of the six blocks near the New Orleans Mint Building. Everything from antiques to crafts and jewelry to candles can be found here. The dedicated shopper will be rewarded with unique finds and good prices. However, like all flea markets, buyer-beware.

Like almost everywhere in the French Quarter, music can be found from various street performers and scheduled musical events. There is no admission to enter the French Market, although few leave with thinning their wallets at least a little bit.

St. Charles Streetcar

St. Charles Avenue, New Orleans, LA 70119
Tel: 504 248 3900
www.norta.com

While New Orleans has three streetcar lines, only the St. Charles Avenue Line can boast being the oldest continuously operated streetcar line in the world. The beautiful streetcars are national historic landmarks and have been running up and down St. Charles Avenue for over 150 years.

The length of the entire line is a 13.2 miles (21.2 kilometers) stretch that takes you past sights including the Central Business District, the Garden District, two universities (Loyola and Tulane), the Audubon Zoological Gardens, and countless historic monuments and mansions.

The scenery is beautiful, but the streetcars are the real stars of the show. Each historic car has brass fittings and mahogany seats. Whether you are rolling along oak lined streets or passing gorgeous antebellum mansions, traveling through town in the streetcars reminds you that the automobile wasn't always king.

The fare on the St. Charles Streetcar Line is $1.25. Passes for one to three days are available.

National World War II Museum

945 Magazine Street
New Orleans, LA 70130
Tel: 504 527 6088
www.ddaymuseum.org

The history presented here may be more recent than much of the other history visitors to the Crescent City soak up just walking around, but it is no less spectacular. This collection of everything from warplanes to General Eisenhower's back-up speech in case the D-Day invasion of Normand failed, present a moving and interesting tour through one of America's greatest hours in the heart of the Warehouse District.

The museum sprung from the genius of Stephen Ambrose, who spent much of his career in New Orleans. The museum is not just for military or history buffs. The complex includes a Tom Hanks produced film called, "Beyond All Boundaries" and is advertised as a 4-D experience. Other attractions are an observation deck to get a better look at some of the real warplanes hanging from the ceiling, the Stage Door Canteen that has live entertainment with 1940's themes, and celebrity chef John Besh's two restaurants.

The exhibits are a mixture of murals, displays, and audio and video presentations, including oral and video histories of veterans. Volunteer veterans can sometimes be found at the museum sharing their stories in person. Many galleries and exhibits have personal effects of soldiers as well.

The museum takes several hours to go through. Several traveling and special galleries and exhibits can be found at the museum at any one time. The museum is family friendly, but some of the movies may be too gruesome for younger children.

General Admission is $21. There are discounts to children, students, and military personnel. World War II veterans are free.

New Orleans Museum of Art (NOMA)

One Collins Diboll circle, City Park
New Orleans, LA 70124
Tel: 504 658 4100
www.noma.org

Located in the Esplanade Ridge section of Mid-City in the middle of City Park, NOMA, as it is commonly known, sits in elegant splendour. The oldest art museum in the city, NOMA houses an impressive array of over 40,000 objects.

Works by masters such as Monet, Renoir, Picasso, Rodin, Gaugin, Pollock, and O'Keeffe are housed here. The extensive European and American works on display here would be worth the visit alone.

Visitors can also find works as varied as pre-Columbian art and Chinese ceramics. The excellent Faberge egg collection is a visitor favourite. A large sculpture garden located behind the mind building provides for viewing modern sculptures among winding trails, magnolias, and bridges over lagoons.

The main building, erected in 1911, creates an impressive and intriguing welcome to the treasures inside. Visiting the museum can be a nice diversion to escape either the sweltering summers or inclement weather.

Guided tours are available if you don't want to just wander around the splendid exhibits. NOMA is open Tuesday through Sunday. General Admission is $10, but free for everyone on Wednesdays.

City Park

Mid-City
www.neworleanscitypark.com

Larger than New York's Central Park, this urban oasis is the jewel of Mid-City. There is plenty to do and see here, even if you only want to wander the tree-lined paths and view the many sculptures and footbridges. The varied attractions within the park run the gamut from athletics to pure amusement.

City Park boasts professional quality golf courses, a stadium, a tennis centre, softball diamonds, soccer fields, and a track that was the 1992 U.S. Olympic teams practice track. Boat and bike rentals are also available. Ridding lessons can be purchased at the Equest Farm, the equestrian stable and farm that is the home to the New Orleans Police Department's stables.

Carousel Gardens Amusement Park is open seasonally. This small amusement park is aimed at younger children; there are no daredevil rollercoasters. However, kids of all ages will enjoy the traditional rides such as bumper cars, a Ferris Wheel, and the 1906 wooden carousel. The antique carousel is listed on the National Register of Historic Places, and is one of only 100 antique wooden carousels left in the United States.

Right next to the amusement park is Storyland. This park was created by some of he city's great parade float makers. The park is filled with scenes and characters from children's literature. The more than twenty-five exhibits include Captain Hook's pirate ship, a dragon, and Jack & Jill's unlucky hill. There is plenty for young ones to see and climb on.

If your group includes an avid gardener or a budding botanist, try visiting the Botanical Garden. This lush collection of over two thousand temperate, semitropical, and tropical plants is for more than just plant lovers. The sprawling thirteen-acre garden is also host to the New Orleans Historic Train Garden.

Admission to the park is free, but the various attractions may charge admission. For the latest information about pricing and seasons of operation about individual attracts visit the City Garden website at: www.neworleanscitypark.com.

Metairie Cemetery

5100 Pontchartrain Blvd.
New Orleans, LA 70124
Tel: 504 486 6331
www.lakelawnmetairie.com

New Orleans has a lot of cemeteries worth visiting. Metairie Cemetery is among the best to visit because of its beauty, history, and the large and varied collection of funeral statuary and monuments.

The cemetery is laid out in an oval layout because it is built on the site of the former Metairie Race Course. Some of the New Orleanians interred here include jazz legends Louis Prima and Al Hirt as well as Confederate General P.G.T. Beauregard. These celebrities are not real the attraction.

The best reason to spend the better part of a day among the dead is the magnificent tombs and monuments. Some of the better-known sights are the Brunswig mausoleum, a pyramid guarded by a sphinx, the Moriarty monument, a sixty-foot tall marble tomb, and the tomb of Josie Arlington, the infamous Stroyville Brothel madam.

Many of the tombs have ornate decorations such as stained glass and ornate sculptures. Many of the sculptures are attractions in their own right, such as the so-called Weeping Angel. Other notable sculptures include two by Alexander Doyle that are part of the Army of Tennessee, Louisiana Division monument, including a stunning statue of General Albert Sydney Johnston on his horse at the top of the tomb.

There is no admission charge to visit the cemetery. Tours can be arranged through several private cemetery tour companies. Self-guided tours are permissible.

Garden District

New Orleans, LA

The well-preserved antebellum mansions perfectly manicured lawns of the Garden District are best seen on foot. It is possible to ride a streetcar or drive through much of the area. However, walking the streets, whether with by ones self or as part of a guided tour, is the only way to soak up all the rich detail of these homes.

This section of the city was originally the separate city of Lafayette. It was settled by Americans after the Louisiana Purchase. The Americans came pouring into the area to take commercial advantage of the Mississippi River and nearby gulf coast. The newcomers and the existing Creole population of the French Quarter took a while to develop a harmonious relationship.

This area displays excellent examples of both early 19th century style architecture and Victorian style architecture. Most of the homes are not open for tours. However, the view from the street is impressive enough for a visit.

There is no charge to walk around the Garden District.

Mississippi River

New Orleans, LA

The greatest river of the United States, and one of the great rivers of the word, Big Muddy, or the Mississippi River, is a sight to behold. Much of New Orleans is actually lower in elevation than the river. The levee system that protects New Orleans is an engineering marvel.

The Mississippi is over 2,400 miles (3,862 kilometers) long. It can be argued that this river is the most important body of water in the United States. A great deal of the nation's commerce still flows between its banks. All of the rain the falls between the Rocky Mountains in the west and the Alleghenies in the east eventually makes its way into the Mississippi and out into the Gulf of Mexico.

The levee protecting the French Quarter is a great place to walk and see the mighty river as it passes by the city on its way to the Gulf of Mexico. Here the river is, on average, 200 feet (60.9 meters) deep. If you are on the levee on a sunny day you are likely to spot several picnickers.

If you want to do more than just see the river, you can take the Canal Street ferry to Algiers Point. The ferry is free to ride and allows you to see how the city was approached for much of its history, from the deck of a ship approaching from the north.

Recommendations for the Budget Traveler

Places to Stay

The price of a hotel room in New Orleans varies more than many cities depending on when you visit. Mardi Gras time is the most expensive time to visit.

French Market Inn

501 Decatur Street, New Orleans, LA 70130
Tel: 1 888 626 2725
www.frenchmarketinn.com

Built in 1832 and located in the center of the French
Quarter, this inn puts you close many of the major
attractions in the city. The building has beautiful
courtyards and gardens. The entire property was
renovated in 2012. There is a round-trip airport shuttle for
a fee.

All rooms include an iron, cable TV, hairdryer, air-
conditioning, the facilities to make your own coffee and
tea. Complimentary high-speed wireless internet access.
Accommodation is priced between $69.00 and $149.99 per
night.

1896 O'Malley House

120 S. Pierce St., New Orleans, LA 70119
Tel: 1 866 226 1896
www.1896omalleyhouse.com

This Mid City Bed and Breakfast is walking distance from
the Canal Street streetcar. The handsome Colonial Revival
residence is decorated with a focus on both authentic
furnishings and comfortable surroundings.

The 1896 O'Malley House has been voted one of the top ten Bed and Breakfasts in the United States. The cozy feel the entire house make it a welcome place to rest after a busy day in the Big Easy.

Rooms vary in size but all include air conditioning, flat screen TV with built-in DVD player, hairdryer, and free wireless high-speed internet access. Expect to pay between $135 and $200 per night.

Lafayette Hotel

600 St. Charles Avenue New Orleans, LA 70130
Tel: 1 888 626 5457
www.lafayettehotelneworleans.com

Located on Lafayette Square, the 1916 hotel has large rooms outfitted with dark woods and antique reproductions. This is a favorite hotel with business travellers because of its proximity to the convention center and many French Quarter sites.

The rooms each have air conditioning, coffee/tea maker, internet access, cable TV, and irons. Rooms vary between $69 and $122 a night.

Bienville House

320 Decatur St., New Orleans, LA 70130
Tel: 1 800 535 7836
www.bienvillehouse.com

Located in the midst of the French Quarter and recently renovated, the Bienville House houses a twenty-four hour salt-water pool. You can step out the door and find the best the French Quarter has to offer. The hotel is also pet friendly. The helpful staff will help with directions and information. Even though there are 83 rooms here, you will feel like you are at a small Bed and Breakfast.

Each room has a four-poster bed. Each room includes coffee/tea maker, hairdryer, clock radio with iPod player, cable/satellite TV, and wireless internet access. Room rates are between $99 to $189 per night.

Andrew Jackson Hotel

919 Royal Street New Orleans, LA 70130
Tel: 1 800 654 0224
www.frenchquarterinns.com/andrewjackson

The attractive yellow and blue façade greets travellers at this traditional choice for French Quarter accommodations. The Victorian style building is in walking distance from Bourbon Street and the French Market. Several of the rooms have wrought iron balconies overlooking Royal Street.

The rooms have ceiling fans, air conditioning, cable TV, and free wireless high-speed internet access. The hotel also offers a complimentary continental breakfast. Accommodations can be found from $80 to $130.

Le Pavillon Hotel

833 Poydras St., New Orleans, LA 70112
Tel: 1 800 535 9095
www.lepavillon.com

The first thing that stands out about this hotel is the amazing lobby. It has classical columns and gorgeous chandeliers. Le Pavillon styles itself as a grand hotel in the style of a bygone era. The hotel is five minutes from the Superdome and two blocks away from the Mardi Gras parade routes.

Expect to pay between $149 to $319 a night for rooms with air conditioning, cable TV, hair dryers, minibar, and free high-speed internet access.

Bourbon Orleans

717 Orleans St., New Orleans, LA 70116
Tel: 1 866 513 9744
www.bourbonorleans.com

With several rooms facing Bourbon Street, this hotel is a great place to see Mardi Gras or other festival parades.

The hotel is a collection of buildings, many dating as far back as he early 1830's. The rooms can vary greatly in size.

Every room features an iron, flat screen TV, clock radio with iPod dock, complimentary bottled water, coffee maker and free high-speed wireless internet access.

Places to Eat

Café du Monde

800 Decatur St., New Orleans, LA 70116
Tel: 800 772 2927
www.cafedumonde.com

Right off Jackson Square, this is perhaps the most famous place for beignets and café au lait in the entire city. You can get a beignet from $2.14 while listening to street performers and watching the world go by on Jackson Square.

This French Market coffee stand traces its roots back to 1862. The café only closes on Christmas Day and for the odd hurricane. There is not much variety on the menu, but what Café du Monde offers, it does well.

Mahony's Po-Boy Shop

3454 Magazine St., New Orleans, LA 70115
Tel: 504 899 3374
www.mahonyspoboys.com

The po'boy is a New Orleans creation. Mahony's offers excellent traditional po'boys as well as modern twists on the working class standard. These fast food sandwiches can be partnered with hand-cut fries and washed down with a beer or soda. A meal here costs between $8 and $21.

Gumbo Shop

630 St. Peter St., New Orleans, LA 70115
Tel: 504 525 1486
www.gumboshop.com

Gumbo is yet another food any visitor to New Orleans must try. The Gumbo at the Gumbo Shop is an excellent introduction to this fabulous Creole classic. If you aren't in the mood for gumbo there is also a fair selection of sandwiches, sides and desserts.

If you choose to have Gumbo you have a wide selection including the award winning Okra Gumbo. You can get a filling meal here for between $8 and $24.

Boucherie

8115 Jeannette St., New Orleans, LA 70118
Tel: 504 862 5514
www.boucherie-nola.com

This may be a little difficult to find, but is worth the effort. The menu changes monthly, but you will not pay more than $16 for an entrée. You will find more types of grits than you thought possible. One of the customer favourites is the Krispy Kreme bread pudding.

Small plates start as low as $5. The proprietors of Boucherie also operate a food truck. The food is a combination of southern styles and Cajun techniques.

Acme Oyster & Seafood Restaurant

725 Iberville St., New Orleans, LA 70130
Tel: 504 835 6410
www.acmeoyster.com

This always crowded seafood eatery is known for raw oysters on the half-shell. The shrimp and fish are also excellent. The red beans and rice is one of the best non-seafood choices on the menu. This French Quarter favorite has a variety of desserts to indulge in after you satisfy your seafood cravings. A meal here will cost between $7 and $23.

Places to Shop

Antiques

New Orleans is city that lives and breathes history. It is also a great place to find and buy pieces of history. Antiques are difficult to buy at a fair price unless you know what you are doing. However vacation and shopping are also about fun. Shopping for antiques in New Orleans is fun, even if you don't buy anything.

Brass Monkey

407 Royal St., French Quarter, New Orleans, LA, 70130
Tel: 504 561 0688

Greg's Antiques

1209 Decatur St, New Orleans, LA 70116
Tel: 504 202 8577

Bush Antiques

2109 Magazine St., Garden District,
New Orleans, LA, 70130
Tel: 504 581 3518

Brass Monkey has many unique walking sticks. Greg's
Antiques has some of the best prices of any of the antique
stores in town, sometimes you can haggle to get an even
better deal. Bush Antiques has items both large and small
and is a great place to find religious artifacts.

French Market

1008 North Peters Street, New Orleans, LA 70116
Tel: 504 522 2621

The open-air flea market and hundreds of small shops
provide for an excellent chance to find the perfect gift for
the friend back home. Don't forget to comparison shop, as
you are likely to find many of the same or similar items at
a variety of price points.

Buffalo Exchange

3312 Magazine St., New Orleans, LA 70115
Tel: 504 891 7443
www.buffaloexchange.com

This vintage and used clothing store is just the place to get outfitted for one of the many costume parties in the city. The key word at this establishment is exchange. While you are free to pay cash, you can also trade-in clothing or accessories for cash or new-to-you merchandise. You can call ahead to see what the proprietors are currently in the market for.

Printed in Great Britain
by Amazon